Anonymus

Annual report - American Society for the Prevention of Cruelty to Animals

Anonymus

Annual report - American Society for the Prevention of Cruelty to Animals

ISBN/EAN: 9783741141041

Manufactured in Europe, USA, Canada, Australia, Japa

Cover: Foto ©Thomas Meinert / pixelio.de

Manufactured and distributed by brebook publishing software
(www.brebook.com)

Anonymus

Annual report - American Society for the Prevention of Cruelty to Animals

AMERICAN SOCIETY

FOR THE

Prevention of Cruelty to Animals.

INCORPORATED BY THE STATE OF NEW YORK.

SEVENTH ANNUAL REPORT.

1873.

HEADQUARTERS OF THE SOCIETY,
FOURTH AVENUE, CORNER OF TWENTY-SECOND STREET,
New York.

NOTICE.

The Secretary respectfully requests subscribers, members, and others, to transmit to the Society's Headquarters, any extracts from newspapers or other publications, which may come under their observation, concerning the objects of the Society, and also all BOOKS treating on Natural History, or of any kind, which may add to the value of the

LIBRARY OF THE SOCIETY,

thereby greatly aiding the Executive Officers in arriving at exact conclusions upon the various subjects which come under their cognizance.

HEADQUARTERS OF THE AMERICAN SOCIETY FOR THE PREVENTION OF CRUELTY TO ANIMALS,
Corner of Fourth Avenue and Twenty-second Street, New York City.

1873.

Officers of the Society,

ELECTED AT THE
ANNUAL MEETING IN MAY.

President.
HENRY BERGH.

Vice-Presidents.

William H. Aspinwall,
Henry W. Bellows,
James Brown,
Horace B. Claflin,
Peter Cooper,

John A. Dix,
Benjamin D. Hicks,
John T. Hoffman,
Marshall O. Roberts,
Moses Taylor.

Executive Committee.

Charles L. Anthony,
N. M. Beckwith,
John M. Bixby,
Thomas C. Doremus,
Nathan C. Ely,
Elbridge T. Gerry,
Townsend Harris,

Charles Lanier,
Frank Leslie,
Charles H. Marshall,
Edward Matthews,
Royal Phelps,
James Stokes,
Alfred Schermerhorn,

Alexander Van Rensselaer.

Treasurer.
Henry Clews.

Counsel.
Elbridge T. Gerry.

Secretary.
N. P. Hosack.

Veterinary Surgeons.

Charles C. Grice.   Alex. F. Liautard.

Honorary Members.

Ulysses S. Grant, President of the United States, *ex-officio.*

Schuyler Colfax, Ex-Vice-President of the United States, *ex-officio.*

John T. Hoffman, Ex-Governor of the State of New York, *ex-officio.*

A. S. Beach, Ex-Lieut.-Governor of the State of New York, *ex-officio.*

Other Ex-Officio Members.

The Right Hon. the Earl of Harrowby, President of the Royal Society for the Prevention of Cruelty to Animals, London.

John Colam, Esq., Secretary for the Royal Society for the P. C. A., London.

Angelo Ames, Esq., of Albany, N. Y.

CHARTER

AN ACT *to incorporate the* AMERICAN SOCIETY FOR THE PREVENTION OF CRUELTY TO ANIMALS. *Passed April 10, 1866, by the Legislature of the State of New York.—Vol. I., Chap.* 469, *Page* 1019 *of the Revised Statutes.*

SEC. 1. That John T. Hoffman, Henry Grinnell, J. J. Astor, Jr., Geo. Bancroft, Shepherd Knapp, James T. Brady, John A. Dix, Marshall O. Roberts, James Brown, Horatio Potter, Thos. H. Taylor, Erastus Brooks, Chas. P. Daly, Moses Taylor, Geo. T. Trimble, John D. Wolfe, Henry W. Bellows, Peter Cooper, Francis B. Cutting, Wm. H. Aspinwall, John Van Buren, Hamilton Fish, Daniel Parish, John J. Cisco, A. Oakey Hall, John McCloskey, Wm. C. Bryant, Edward G. Steele, Horace Greeley, Samuel B. Ruggles, James Lenox, August Belmont, Moses H. Grinnell, Wm. H. Webb, Jas. Gallatin, Harper Brothers, Jas. J. Roosevelt, C. V. S. Roosevelt, Alex. Stuart, D. C. Kingsland, Jas. W. Gerard, Joseph P. Beach, Geo. T. Olyphant, Oliver S. Strong, Henry Clews, Archibald Russell, Benjamin R. Winthrop, John A. Kennedy, Daniel Carpenter, Geo. W. Dilks, Chas. Addoms, Geo. Griswold, Simeon Draper, Robert L. Stewart, Andrew Warner, Alex. T. Stewart, Daniel Butterfield, A. C. Kingsland, E. A. Washburn, M. S. Beach, John D. Jones, Frank Leslie, Wm. Coventry H. Waddell, Chas. A. Bristed, Thos. C. Acton, Wm.

McMurray, James Leonard, A. D. Russell, Henry Bergh, all of the city of New York, and such other persons as may be associated with them, in conformity to this act, and their successors, are hereby constituted and created a body corporate, by the name of " The American Society for the Prevention of Cruelty to Animals."

SEC. 2. The officers of the said corporation shall consist of a president, ten vice-presidents, one secretary, one treasurer, an executive committee of fifteen members, and such other officers as shall from time to time seem necessary to this Society.

SEC. 3. The foregoing officers shall be chosen from among the members of the Society.

SEC. 4. A library may be created for the use of the Society.

SEC. 5. The said Society, for fixing the terms of admission of its members, for the government of the same, for the election, changing, and altering the officers above named, and for the general regulation and management of its affairs, shall have power to form a code of By-Laws, not inconsistent with the laws of this State or of the United States, which code, when formed and adopted at a regular meeting, shall, until modified or rescinded, be equally binding as this act, upon the Society, its officers and members.

SEC. 6. This Society shall not, in its corporate capacity, hold real estate exceeding in value, at any one time, the sum of one hundred thousand dollars.

SEC. 7. The police force of the city of New York, as well as of all other places where police organizations exist, shall, as occasion may require, aid the Society, its members, or agents, in the enforcement of all laws which are now, or may hereafter be, enacted for the protection of dumb animals.

Sec. 8. One-half of the fines collected through the instrumentality of the Society, or of its agents, for violations of such laws, shall accrue to the benefit of said Society.

Sec. 9. The provisions of this act shall be general, within the boundaries of the State.

Sec. 10. This act shall take effect immediately.

AMENDMENT OF CHARTER.

An Act relative to the acquisition of real property by the American Society for the Prevention of Cruelty to Animals, and to amend the Charter thereof. Passed 7th March, 1871.

The People of the State of New York, represented in Senate and Assembly, do enact as follows:

Sec. 1. The American Society for the Prevention of Cruelty to Animals, a Corporation created by an Act of the Legislature of this State, passed April 10th, 1866, is hereby authorized and empowered to take, hold, use and enjoy all the lands, tenements and hereditaments which were by the last will of Louis Bonard devised unto the said Corporation, for the uses and purposes in said will expressed. And all the estate, claim, right, title and interest of the people of this State, of, in and to said lands, tenements and hereditaments, and every part thereof, are hereby released, granted, confirmed to and vested in said Corporation.

SEC. 2. The Sixth Section of an act entitled "An Act to incorporate the American Society for the Prevention of Cruelty to Animals," passed April tenth, eighteen hundred and sixty-six, is hereby amended, and shall read as follows:

SEC. 6. This Corporation shall be capable of taking, holding and enjoying any real property by virtue of any deed, or of any devise contained in any last will of any person whomsoever, subject to the provisions of law relative to devises by last will. But this Corporation shall not, in its corporate capacity, hold real estate the yearly income derived from which shall exceed the sum of fifty thousand dollars.

SEC. 3. Nothing in this act contained shall in any manner affect the right of any heir or creditor of the late Louis Bonard.

SEC. 4. This act shall take effect immediately.

ANNUAL MEETING

OF THE

AMERICAN

Society for the Prevention of Cruelty to Animals.

1873.

HEADQUARTERS OF THE SOCIETY,
COR. FOURTH AVENUE AND TWENTY-SECOND STREET,
NEW YORK, 17th May, 1873.

THE Annual Meeting of the Society was held at its
Headquarters, corner of Fourth Avenue and Twenty-
second street, this evening; the President, Henry Bergh,
presiding, who opened the proceedings with the following Report and remarks:

LADIES AND GENTLEMEN:

The termination of another year, introduces us to the
seventh anniversary of the existence of the parent society in America, created for the protection of the
defenceless brute creation from cruelty. It would be as
difficult to enumerate the benefits which have resulted
from its past existence, as to predict its future usefulness. One fact, however, may be adduced, tending to
assist in arriving at an approximate estimate of the

former, viz.: that twenty-five States and territories of
our country, including Canada, approving and admiring
our example, have founded similar societies, and generally
adopted for their shield the emblem of this one. That
there remains ample work for all of us, the observation
of every humane person confirms ; nor is this conclusion
reached merely by reason of the overt cruelties which
force themselves on the public view, but by the equally
significant evidence afforded through the utterances of
public thought. There are many intelligent persons who,
while admitting that it is a great wrong to cruelly treat
a horse, an ox, a dog, or other useful domestic animal, completely deny to creatures still lower in animal
life all consideration, and claim it as a privilege, if not
a duty, to manifest their aversion, by the infliction of
tortures which betray, to say the least, an imperfect
civilization. They fail to appreciate the full significance
of the sentiment of humanity, which regards the infliction of needless pain and suffering, even on the meanest
and most obnoxious living thing, still as cruelty ; and,
as such, an insult to that omnipotent Power, whose
greatest attributes are indiscriminate mercy and com-
passion to all His creatures.

" Why," remarked a Senator, while our bill was under
consideration in that branch of the legislature, during
the present session—" why, these humanitarians will by-
and-bye tell us that we should be tender in the treatment of the rat, the reptile, and the bug! "

Yes, Mr. Senator, you are right ; only your prediction
is not comprehensive enough ; for the " by-and-bye " is
now present, ever has been, and ever will be, because it
is an attribute of the Deity and of His world. Kill, if
necessary, but torture not, is the command of intelligent
reason. While on this subject of

LEGISLATION,

it is best to dispose of it here. A bill entitled "An Act
for the better prevention of disease and cruelty," was
carefully prepared by Mr. Gerry and myself, and early
introduced to the Senate. The medium of its presenta-
tion was unfortunate; for Senator Benedict, to whom
it was given in charge, soon betrayed a strong aversion
to, and opposed it with a ceaseless persistency, which, if
exercised in a right direction, would soon earn for him a
lasting fame. But, however violent the opposition which
proceeded from this source, it was in the Judiciary Committee that it was destined to experience an opposition,
not alone, as in the former instance, characterized by an
inconsiderate antipathy, but by an open, undisguised
hostility, based seemingly on personal and pecuniary
interests alone, on the part of one of its members.

The principal opposition which it received was to the
section prohibiting the salting of the streets, for the purpose of melting snow and ice, a practice most disastrous
to the feet of horses and the health of human beings. A
large deputation of railroad and omnibus proprietors
from New York and Brooklyn appeared before the Judiciary Committee of the Senate, to which it was referred,
who warmly advocated its use, and were as earnestly opposed by ourselves and the expert testimony which we
produced, among which latter was that of Dr. Sayer,
late health officer of this port. During this discussion an
incident occurred which afforded painful evidence of the
habitual disregard of the amenities of official intercourse
which characterizes, as a rule, the deliberations of many
of our public bodies. An illiterate fellow, proprietor of one of the omnibus lines of this city, accompanied
by his dull but malicious legal adviser, thinking that he
was addressing his associates of the stable and the " Sample

Room," gave vent to a string of falsehood and invective against myself which, while it was certainly actionable at law, was far too low and disgusting for notice. Pre-eminently vile as was this tirade, and that of his paid companion, it will amaze all respectable readers to learn that they were permitted to thus violate the established usages of parliamentary decorum, by the employment of the grossest personalities, unrebuked! And yet there were on that committee two or three able and worthy gentlemen who silently tolerated the insult thus offered them! It soon became apparent that in order to pro-gress the bill, all contained within it which in the least affected the railroad interests must be eliminated; and this having been accordingly done, assurance was given by the senator from Kings county representing these interests, that no further opposition would proceed from that quarter. Conceive our surprise, however, on finding that every remaining provision of the bill received the most determined assault from the same source while under discussion in committee of the whole; and ulti-mately, while on its final passage, in order to try and kill it with a single blow, he moved "that the enacting clause be stricken out." It is gratifying to report, how-ever, that this unbecoming struggle to destroy a most useful and humane measure failed by a vote of 18 to 5.

In nearly a similar case, which has just come to my knowledge, the House of Representatives refused to allow a member to vote on account of his personal in-terest in a subject about to be voted on.

While thus communicating to the Society, as is my duty, every thing antagonistic to its proceedings, it be-comes me, as well, to speak in appreciative terms of the steadfast and statesmanlike action of Gen. D. P. Wood, the faithful and laborious chairman of the Judiciary

Committee of the Senate ; who, insensible to the clamor
of some of his colleagues, supported, with his sympathy
and commanding talents, every provision of the bill
until the end. I feel assured that this Society will share
my feelings of gratitude toward this excellent gentleman, to whom we are mainly indebted for its triumphant
passage through the Senate.

Mr. Gerry having appeared before the Judiciary Committee of the Assembly, and explained our bill, it was
reported favorably by the Chairman, Mr. Prince, and on
the evening of March 13 it was advanced out of its
regular order and considered. Although much opposition was manifested, it was evident, as the Speaker and
other gentlemen subsequently remarked to me, that the
feeling of the House was decidedly favorable to it.

True to his former practice and instincts, the person
who is usually designated as "the member from Sligo,"
arrayed himself fiercely against it, in obedience to his
pet idiosyncrasy, to wit : That criminals shall be arrested
only "on warrant." The practical operation of this idea
is worthy of illustration. If you see a man beating out
the brains of a hard-working horse, for example, you must
step up to the offender and request him, after he shall
have sufficiently satisfied his vengeance, to give you his
address, if he have any, or if not, then to remain where he
is for a few hours, until you can go and find a magis-
trate and obtain a warrant, when you may arrest him,
provided he has been sufficiently obliging to await your
return. On the 18th of March it was "moved" by Mr.
Batcheller, of Saratoga ; and after several injurious
amendments had been made to it, further discussion was
deferred until the evening of the 20th inst., when
it was made the special order for that occasion ; and
after the canal interest had stricken out all protection

to its toiling and tortured skeletons of horses, and
the butchers, and the slaughterers of birds and fowls
"for the fun of the thing," in contests of skill for a
wager, had each satisfied their pet cruelty, Mr. C. G.
Cornell, of this city, also offered an "amendment"
that no arrest should be made except on warrant first
obtained! I need not detain you by any further
comments on this impracticable measure, the tendency of
which, as you are aware, is to speedily consign the living,
practical, and active institution which your humanity
sustains, into one of those effete and musty curiosities,
with which the museum of neglected laws abounds.
Nor will I do the intelligence of the mover of it the in-
justice to believe that even he thinks it reasonable and
practicable! No; the simple purpose of the mover of the
amendment was to hopelessly cripple, if not destroy, the
beneficent usefulness of this Society, and gain for himself the applause and suffrages of those among his con-
stituents who are always the recognized enemies of society at large. After a few more inconsiderable "amendments," as they are facetiously termed, the bill was
ordered to a "third reading," and finally, on the 20th of
March, the Senate bill, No. 95, was reached, and, not-
withstanding the numerous "amendments" it had received in its passage through both Houses, it was
ultimately "killed" by a vote of 58 nays to 52 ayes—
absent 18.

The innocent outside world may well be astonished at
this, but the inside citizen feels no emotion of that sort,
being familiar with machinery and engineering in general. In short, it was boldly asserted on the previous
evening that the railroad and omnibus philanthropists
had sent up the necessary quantity of oil to make the
engine run quietly; and hence, this bill, along with one
or two others obnoxious to those unselfish patriots, and

put together in the same pool, was ground to powder!
On the announcement of the vote, the vigilant and friendly Husted obtained a resolution laying it on the table,
with a view to its future consideration, and after
thanking our friends, Mr. Gerry and I took the first
train to town.

On the 14th of this month, Mr. Husted moved to re-
consider the vote by which our bill was lost, when Mr.
C. S. Lincoln, of Ontario, opposed the motion.

LOUIS BONARD'S ESTATE.

It is with infinite pleasure that I announce to you the
final termination of the tedious " Bonard Will Case,"
which has obtained for itself a distinction which gives
it high rank among the *causes celebres* of the courts
of posthumous justice. My experiences during this
equivocal contest have not elevated my opinions of the
moral superiority of the " superior animal " over the
lower. So far as I have observed, those humble creatures
whose protection we assume, never exhibit in their intercourse with one another a higher order of selfishness and
avarice, than most of the learned beings have betrayed
in their relations to this inquiry. But, however conspicuous these characteristics have appeared during the
inquisition itself, it was reserved for the adjustment of
the pecuniary claims to make the disparity more so.

I should consume too much of your time, and per-
chance too greatly disturb your equanimity, by detailing
these subtle and absorbing efforts to divert from its
legitimate use, the generous bequest of the good Mr.
Bonard. Suffice it to say that the ingenuity of counsel,
along with the extravagant demands of medical ex-
perts(?), succeeded in relieving the estate of about
$30,000. In the former connection, however, I do not
mean to include the legitimate professional services of

the learned and honorable gentleman representing the principal contestants, Judge John K. Porter.

The antithesis of all this selfishness is furnished in the person of the able gentleman who presides over the legal interests of the Society,

MR. ELBRIDGE T. GERRY.

To his eminent professional abilities, zeal, perseverance, and devotion to this God-approving work of defending the defenseless, the Society and its cause owe a debt inappreciable in dollars. I think that if I had ever been skeptical of the eternal presence of an overruling Providence in the affairs of this world, my repeated experiences in the progress of this work would alone suffice to extinguish all doubt. How often, during its inception and development, have the dark clouds which lowered over my path suddenly and most unexpectedly opened, and the aid and support so coveted, and which rendered me for the time so despondent, have cleared them away. I regard this excellent gentleman as a signal manifestation of that Divine Sovereignty to which I allude. Not only have his prudent and sagacious counsels prevented or parried harm, but by his eloquent and astute advocacy of the rights of the Society before the judicial tribunals of the State, he has in some instances affirmed its powers, and preserved to its treasury that material element of success which, it is my melancholy duty to record, has prompted so many able yet selfish contestants to endeavor to divert from its sacred and humane destination, to their own personal uses. His skill and industry, however, were not sufficient to avert a loss of some thirty thousand dollars to the bequest of Mr. Bonard, all consumed in claims, court charges, and allowances to counsel—with one single exception—for the appreciable service of having stopped the realization of the dead man's holy desire for the space of more than two years!

INJUNCTIONS.

It has become the practice of late, on the part of corporations, to have recourse to this legal panacea, when their actions will not bear the scrutiny of an ordinary trial. Injunctions and orders to show cause, possess one captivating merit: they enable those obtaining them to suspend the operation of law, while dismal and deferred argument " drags its slow length along." Five of the unselfish stage proprietors of this city have procured this blessing against us, in part; and two large abattoirs have been equally successful in their petition to be allowed to murder, in horrible agonies, the unoffending brute destined for human food !

EPIZOOTIC.

During the past year a disease thus characterized has visited our country with the most fatal results ; but, like most of the misfortunes of this life, it carried along with it an instructive moral ; for it painfully illustrated to the world the value of the horse, and how directly dependent mankind are on that glorious animal. I wish the thoughtless would pause a moment to consider : if the partial loss of the usefulness of one race of animals can so disturb all the relations of life, what would be the consequence if we were suddenly deprived of all the inferior animals ! Could a deluge or an earthquake produce more terrible results?

WASTE OF ANIMAL LIFE.

As is well known to the Society, we have undertaken the destruction of all animals irrecoverably disabled, in order to insure them a speedy and merciful death. Our officers during the past year have killed 835 horses, exclusive of smaller animals. The Police Department has resigned this duty into our hands, and regularly notifies us whenever wanted.

I think that my observations abroad and at home justify me in saying that in no other part of the world is animal life esteemed so cheaply. It is asserted that some street-railroad proprietors act on the principle that horseflesh is cheaper than good oats ; and hence it pays better to run these wretched animals so long as any vitality remains in them, and then replace them by others. But it is not only this class of proprietors that are open to this cruel censure; those engaged in the transportation of animals from a distance, swell the fearful sacrifice, as has lately been shown, by fifteen hundred at a time perishing of cold and starvation ! Even exhibitors of rare and costly creatures, have furnished their quota to the tremendous catalogue; and you doubtless all remember the late appalling destruction of Mr. Barnum's menagerie, for the third time. Now, I do not hesitate to say that all these awful disasters are the result of carelessness, and a defective system of confining the creatures they have in charge. With scarce an exception, they are kept in places wholly unsuited for the purpose. While in transit they are far less protected than inanimate freight; and, when stationary, are shut up in buildings which only serve as fagots to roast them alive. Among the provisions of the bill which we presented to the Legislature was a remedy for these inhuman occurrences.

MISCELLANEOUS.

I have petitioned the Mayor and Common Council, to provide us with a lot of ground and a suitable building, for the merciful destruction of the suffering vagrant dogs wandering about the streets, with an offer on our part to take charge of this work, free of other expense to the city government. The subject was referred to the Committee on Public Works, who reported that although they were in favor of the plan, they did not know of any appropriation from which funds could be drawn or used for carrying out the object suggested.

Continued appeals to the Federal Congress have resulted in the passage of an act regulating the transportation of cattle from State to State.

The substitution of steam engines for horses propelling street cars and canal boats is still under consideration.

THE NEW HEADQUARTERS OF THE SOCIETY.

In conclusion, I have to congratulate the Society on its acquisition of permanent quarters for the transaction of its business. During the seven years of our official existence, we have contentedly, although at much inconvenience, transacted our business at a great disadvantage. To those who are familiar with the immense proportions to which this work has grown, the demand for increased space will not be surprising.

In a word, from nothing it has spread its humanizing influence over our whole country, and called into being societies for the protection of the inferior animals, where none ever existed before.

Again, the dignity of the work, as well as the immensity of its achievements, warrant the society in the judicious purchase of the elegant and commodious building it now possesses.

Mr. Nathan C. Ely moved the following resolution, which was seconded and carried unanimously :

Resolved, That the admirable address of the President of the Society be, and is hereby, highly approved of, and he is requested to cause the same to be published.

The Chairman then called upon the Acting-Secretary to read the minutes of the last meeting of the Society. which were as follows:

At a special meeting of the " American Society for the Prevention of Cruelty to Animals," held on the 7th May, 1873, in accordance with Chapter XIX. of the Code of By-Laws, Mr. Elbridge T. Gerry proposed, in writing, the following Amendments to the Code of By-Laws of the Society:

> 1. Amend Section 4 of Chapter IV. of the Code of By-Laws so that the same shall read as follows:

§ 4. The fiscal year of the Society shall, for all purposes, commence on the first day of January, and end with the thirty-first day of December, in each year.

> 2. Amend Section 2 of Chapter V. of the Code of By-Laws so that the same shall read as follows:

§ 2. The officers of the Society shall be chosen from among its members. With the exception of the Superintendent, who shall be appointed by, and hold office during the pleasure of, the President, they shall be elected every three years by ballot, and shall hold their offices respectively until others are elected in their places. Such election shall take place at the annual meeting of the Society, in the year when it falls due, and if from any cause there shall be a failure of such election at the time above mentioned, the same may be held at a meeting to be specially called for that purpose, in a manner specified in the Seventh Chapter of this Code of By-Laws.

3. Amend Sections 1 and 2 of Chapter VI. of the Code of By-Laws so that the same shall read as follows, respectively :

§ 1. The annual meeting of the Society shall be held on the first Thursday in January, or as soon thereafter as convenient, in each and every year hereafter.

§ 2. Every member of the Society who has been such for Twenty days or more, and who is not in arrears for his dues, shall be entitled to vote at any election.

4. Amend Section 2 of Chapter VII. of the Code of By-Laws so that the same shall read as follows:

§ 2. Such call shall be made by keeping posted a notice of the time and place of such meeting in a conspicuous place in the office or rooms of the Society, during at least two days before the same is proposed to be held.

5. Amend Section 11 of Chapter XVII. of the Code of By-Laws so that the same shall read as follows:

§ 11. At all meetings of the Executive Committee, three members present shall constitute a quorum for the transaction of business.

Adjourned.

HENRY BERGH.

The foregoing amendments were adopted by a unanimous vote of the members present.

T. W. HARTFIELD,
Acting Secretary.

The Chairman then called upon the Acting Secretary to read the Reports of the Secretary, Executive Committee, and Treasurer.

Secretary's Report.

The Secretary presents the following Report of the general work of the Society, its Branches and Agents, for the past year.

LECTURES.

During the year the President has received a large number of urgent invitations to visit various parts of the country, and, by delivering lectures and addresses, aid in the formation of kindred Societies for the prevention of Cruelty to Animals. Pressing calls from far-off cities in many States where as yet the flag of protection is not unfurled, have been declined by the President, owing to his incessant labors in our own city, but in such cases letters of advice, accompanied by documents, have been forwarded, and good results have followed.

The following places have been visited and lectures delivered by the President:

1872, May 3. Jersey City.—First anniversary of the Hudson County Society for the Prevention of Cruelty to Animals.

1872, May 23. Sing Sing.—At the organization of a Branch of the Society at that place.

1872, Nov. 27. Auburn, N. Y.—By invitation of the Young Men's Christian Association at that place.

1872, Dec. 18. Providence, R. I.—By invitation of the Rhode Island Society for the Prevention of Cruelty to Animals.

1873, Jan. 17. New York City.—Plympton Hall, by request of the New York Liberal Club.

1873, March. Trenton, N. J.—At the organization of a Branch of the New Jersey Society.

1873, April. Paterson, N. J.—By invitation of the Passaic County Society for the Prevention of Cruelty to Animals.

SPREAD OF THE HUMANE WORK.

The American Society for the Prevention of Cruelty to Animals has, in addition to its local staff, fifty-four agents in various parts of the State, engaged in carrying on its humane labor, and the reports recently received from them are very satisfactory. In towns and villages where the most outrageous acts of cruelty were of frequent occurrence, hardly a single case has occurred during the past year. The knowledge that an Agent, wearing his shield of office, is near, and that sure and speedy punishment will follow, prevents the infliction of much suffering. The Society has also ten regularly organized Branches in full working order.

The following statement shows the steady progress of the good work:

Alabama.—No laws.
Arkansas.—No laws.
California.—Laws passed and two Societies organized.
Connecticut.—Laws before the Legislature—Society organized and charter granted.
Delaware.—In correspondence with the American Society.
Florida.—No laws.
Georgia.—Laws passed and State Society organized.
Illinois.—Laws passed and State Society organized.

Indiana.—City of Indianapolis, ordinances passed and put in force.

Iowa.—Laws passed and State Society organized.

Kansas.—No laws.

Kentucky.—Laws passed and State Society organized.

Louisiana.—No laws.

Maine.—Laws passed and two Societies organized.

Massachusetts.—Laws passed, State Society and three Branches organized.

Maryland.—Laws passed and State Society organized.

Michigan.—Laws passed and State Society organized.

Minnesota.—Laws passed and State Society organized.

Mississippi.—No laws.

Missouri.—Laws passed and State Society organized.

Nebraska.—No laws.

Nevada.—No laws.

New Hampshire.—Laws passed and two Societies organized.

New Jersey.—Laws passed and four Societies organized.

New York.—Laws passed, State Society and ten Branches.

North Carolina.—Laws passed and State Society organized.

Ohio.—Laws passed and four Societies organized.

Oregon.—Laws passed and State Society organized.

Pennsylvania.—Laws passed and four Societies organized.

Rhode Island.—Laws passed and two Societies organized.

South Carolina.—No laws.

Tennessee.—Laws passed and State Society organized.

Texas.—Laws passed and State Society organized.

Vermont.—In correspondence with the American Society.

Virginia.—Organization being effected.

West Virginia.—Laws passed and State Society organized.

Wisconsin.—No laws.

TERRITORIES.

Alaska.—No laws.

Arizona.—No laws.

Colorado.—Laws passed and State Society organized.

Dakota.—No laws.

Idaho.—No laws.

Indian.—No laws.

Montana.—No laws.

New Mexico.—No laws.

Utah.—No laws.

Washington.—No laws.

Wyoming.—No laws.

D. Columbia—Washington.—Laws passed and Society organized.

CANADA.

Ottawa.—Society organized.

Montreal.—Two societies organized.

Quebec.—Society organized.

PROSECUTIONS.

During the past twelve months the Society have prosecuted 561 cases of cruelty to animals, as detailed in the tabular statement on page 22. Of these, many were of the most heartless character, as the following proves :

Thos. Herne, for working a poor, old horse before a loaded dirt cart, in a diseased condition. Fined twenty-five dollars.

John McQuire, for an atrocious act of cruelty to a mare, out of revenge to the owner. Three months' imprisonment.

JAMES O'HARO, for beating his horse with a heavy cart-rung. Five days, city prison.

GEORGE PALMER (a veterinary surgeon), for abandoning a sick horse in the street for two days and nights. Fined twenty-five dollars.

PHILIP GENNER, working a horse with sores under the harness—second arrest. Five days, city prison.

DAVID M. KEILER, for compelling four horses to draw three New Haven steam passenger cars, weighing over fifty tons, from the Forty-second street depot. Fined twenty dollars.

BERNARD KEIRNAN, working a sick horse—third time arrested. Ten days' imprisonment.

PETER HOWARD, for beating an overloaded horse with a heavy board over the head and body. Ten days' imprisonment.

JOHN COLLINS, for fracturing a horse's jaw with a heavy cart-rung. One month's imprisonment.

The Buffalo Branch of the Society reports the following terrible catalogue of cases prosecuted in one year:

Cases of cruelty of various kinds prevented by personal intervention,	1000	
Whole No. of prosecutions,	87	
Working sick and disabled animals,	44	
Cruelly beating horses,	5	
Dragging an ox by a rope tied around his leg,	1	
Dog fighting,	4	
Leaving poultry on the ground with feet tied,	1	
Failing to provide proper food and shelter for animals,	1	
Pouring boiling tar on a dog,	1	
A car-driver for driving into a flock of sheep,	1	
Using a horse with a broken leg,	1	
Overloading,	6	
Overdriving,	11	
Underfeeding,	1	
Shooting match,	1	
Exhibition of cock-fighting,	1	
Malicious cutting and disabling of cows,	2	
Dragging cow by the neck,	1	
Leaving a cow with a broken leg on a railroad track four days,	1	
Carrying calves with legs tied,	1	
Drawing a sick horse by a chain around the neck for 2 blocks,	1	
Mutilating a dog,	1	
Keeping cows in filthy stable,	1	

The Agents of our Society have also investigated over one thousand reported cases, and, although the offenders have not been arrested, the evils complained of have been remedied. Great trouble is occasioned by citizens sending anonymous complaints to the Society, and many acts of gross cruelty go unpunished for the want of more definite information. A large number of cases have been abandoned owing to the unwillingness of witnesses to come forward at the trials. Numerous premeditated dog and cock-fights in New York, Brooklyn, and Westchester, have been broken up, and the ruffians dispersed before they had commenced their pastime; 753 sick, lame and disabled horses have been ordered out of harness and sent home to their stables in New York City and Brooklyn alone, and during the prevalence of the horse disease hundreds of the poor suffering creatures were relieved from work. Poor pedlars and vendors, unable to pay for advice and medicine were supplied gratis with both, by the Society and its Veterinary Surgeons.

AMBULANCE WORK.

The ambulances of the Society have been called out on 250 occasions, to remove sick and disabled horses from the streets. The life of many a valuable animal has been saved by means of these useful vehicles, which are loaned gratis, the owner providing the team. They are kept in constant readiness at the headquarters of the Society.

HORSES DESTROYED.

During the past year the officers have destroyed 835 horses in New York and Brooklyn, unfit for further use. Hundreds of smaller animals have also been mercifully disposed of.

THE HORSE EPIDEMIC.

During the prevalence of the dreadful and fatal disease among horses last fall, the Society was placed in a difficult position. For days and weeks hardly a single horse appeared in the streets which was not more or less affected with the distemper, and the poor beasts were in a pitiable condition and manifestly unfit for work. Frequent and urgent appeals were made by citizens and the press, to the Society to stop the street railroad companies from working their horses at all, and in some cases this was done; but where the disease was so general, it soon became apparent, that in order to benefit the animals the whole city travel and business would have to be stopped. The President decided on a middle course, and all horses found in a very bad condition were ordered back to their stables. Letters were written by the Society to the various railroad and stage companies, begging them to suspend travel on Sundays, thereby affording their suffering animals rest. Some of the companies complied and others reduced the number of cars running.

CASES IN ABEYANCE.

The following is a list of cases in which the offenders have been indicted by the Grand Jury, and will be tried :

John Glannon, car-driver on the Bleecker-street railroad, for working a lame horse.

Henry P. and W. F. Niebuhr, for dog-figting.

Samuel T. Warner, Supt. of the Bleecker-street railroad, for driving a horse with a quittor on the foot.

THE EPIZOOTIC OF 1872—Scene representing the Suffering Animals in a Railroad Stable.

William Travis, car-driver on the Bleecker Street Rrilroad, for driving a horse with a quittor on the foot.

Hugh O'Rorke, carrying calves in a cruel manner.

John Powers, cruelly beating calves.

Andrew Waunder, knocking out the eye of an ox.

John Deister, aiding and abetting same.

Patrick Hardy, knocking out the eye of a horse.

James E. Dodd, driving a lame horse before a stage of the Broadway and Fourteenth Street line.

RECORD OF CASES PROSECUTED BY THE SOCIETY, ITS BRANCHES AND AGENTS, IN EACH YEAR.

	1866-67	1867-68	1868-69	1869-70	1870-71	1871-72	1872-73	TOTALS.
For cruelly beating Horses or other Animals with whips, clubs or other weapons,	41	34	50	45	45	36	49	300
For carrying Animals in a cruel or inhuman manner,	10	8	20	25	23	17	28	131
For driving lame, sick or disabled Horses,	15	115	130	149	180	230	302	1121
For overloading or overdriving Horses and Mules,	3	20	11	20	26	26	42	148
For acts of Cruelty to Cattle, Dogs, Cats, Poultry, etc.,	20	30	20	5	24	27	39	165
For Dog or Cock Fighting,		4	6	3		18	64	95
For using Bit Burrs or other instruments of torture,					1	1	11	13
For starving or abandoning Horses or other Animals,	12	11	27	22	13	7	18	110
For maliciously mutilating and wounding Animals with knives, etc.						3	8	11
Totals,	101	222	264	269	312	365	561	2094

GENERAL SUMMARY.

Since the formation of the Society in 1866, it has investigated over five thousand reported cases. Of these two thousand and ninety-four have been prosecuted. The Ambulances of the Society have removed nearly fifteen hundred horses which had fallen sick or injured themselves in the streets.

COCK AND DOG FIGHTS.

These brutal and demoralizing scenes, as before remarked, are of very rare occurrence in this city; but the following is worthy of special notice :

On the 17th of February information reached the Society that a cock fight and rat bait was in progress in a private stable, 230 W. 47th street, owned by a Charles E. Carman. Superintendent Hartfield and officer Evans, of the Society, immediately visited the place and found a party of some twenty well-dressed men assembled in a loft over the stable. All present in the pit were arrested. Three of the "sports" were found hid away in the feedbins. They were arraigned the next morning before Justice Bixby at the Yorkville Police Court. His Honor discharged all except the proprietor, Charles E. Carman, and a man named John Fisher, holding both for trial. They were afterward tried at the Court of Special Sessions, before Judges Shandley, Cox and Coulter. Mr. Henry Bergh prosecuted in person. Carman pleaded guilty and was fined fifty dollars. Fisher was acquitted, although it was clearly proved he was aiding and abetting, and at the time of arrest was actually engaged in removing the gaffs from a dying bird. Owing to the frequent and urgent appeals from the President, the Brooklyn police have arrested several gangs of cock-fighters, and many others have been completely suppressed.

WASTE OF ANIMAL LIFE.

This Company, which is under contract with the city authorities to remove from the streets all dead horses and other animals, as well as meat condemned by the Board of Health, furnishes the following statistics of their work during the past twelve months. Since the 1st of May, 1872, the Company had received:

Dead Horses	.	5,130	Dead Cows	.	232
Live Horses	.	986	Dead Dogs	.	3,027
Farcied Horses	.	720	Dead Cats	.	3,324
Glandered Horses	.	917	Dead Goats	.	215

137,600 barrels Offal.

Of the above 2,575 horses died from the epizootic; 682 were destroyed with rotten feet, caused to a great extent by traveling through the salted streets during the past winter; many others lost their hoofs by reason of the reprehensible practice of throwing nails in the streets; and 210 were received with broken or fractured limbs.

The following statistics from the Company of their business during the prevalence of the late terrible epidemic will be found interesting:

Between the 25th of October and the 18th of November 1,506 horses were received by the Rendering Company, at which period the disease was at its height. Of the total number 246 were received from the car stables, 59 from stage stables, and the balance from private stables—a large proportion of the latter being fine truck or road and carriage horses. Only four mules were received. The highest number reached was on the 9th of November, when 96 dead horses were received on the dock. On the 4th of November 89 were collected. Owing to the want of horses it was found impossible to collect all the dead animals, and a large number had to be buried above One Hundreth street. In cutting up and dissecting the animals, a large number of the poor beasts had all the appearance of having been physicked to death. The Rendering Company were at great expense in fulfilling their contract with the city authorities during this trying period. Their own horses being sick, they had to hire, at the rate of $20 per day, teams to send around the city. Six double trucks, six carts, and two trucks drawn by oxen, were daily at work.

Report of the Executive Committee.

THE Executive Committee of the American Society for the Prevention of Cruelty to Animals, offer their sincere congratulations to the members upon the successful termination of the Bonard Will case. On the 5th of December, the real estate was formally surrendered to the Society, after a detention of two and a half years, and on the 8th of the present month, the final accounting of the receiver was rendered, and a full discharge given by the President as sole executor.

The committee also congratulate the members upon the acquisition of a handsome and convenient building, to serve as the headquarters of the Society. The selection of a building and its adaptation to the requirements of the work we are engaged in, were left entirely to the President, the Committee feeling assured that no one could more thoroughly appreciate the peculiar needs of the Society; and the result is, that to-day the Institution is in possession of a building, which is unquestionably superior in beauty and utility, to all others in existence, employed in the same work. A more particular description thereof is given in this report, with illustration.

CIRCULAR.

With a view to the dissemination of our principles and practice in the cause of brute protection, the following letter was addressed by the President to the Governors of all the States and Territories, and with gratifying results in many instances:

To His Excellency, Governor —— :

Sir : It is a popular axiom, that the civilization of a people is indicated by their treatment of the inferior animals. With the decline and fall of the Greek and Roman Empires, were associated brutal exhibitions, at which wild animals were made to tear each other to pieces for the amusement of patrician and plebeian men and women; until at length, the popular taste required a higher sacrifice, in the slaughter of man by his brother man. Amid these cruel and demoralizing spectacles, the glory and splendor of those States were extinguished, never more to be revived.

As with that epoch of the world's history, so with ours. May not the present wasted and insignificant power and influence of the Spanish people, be traced to the national indulgence of their barbarous taste for bull-fighting ? Here at home, too, in free and progressive America, the seeds of a like decay and dissolution are springing up, to disfigure the virgin soil of our prosperous Republic ; and the thoughtful and patriotic, alive to these fatal consequences, are sounding the note of alarm, and organizing into peaceful bands, throughout the country, with a view to the enacting of laws, and the creation of societies, whose purpose is mercy to Heaven's inferior creatures, which means mercy to mankind as well.

Eighteen States and Territories have already manifested their appreciation of the benefits of such associations ; and I would most earnestly and respectfully request your Excellency, to institute such measures as will best facilitate similar humane intentions within your State ; and to this end, would esteem it a privilege, if, when any person or persons may be discovered willing to take the initiative, I might be communicated with, in order to render their task more easy, through the experience which this Society is capable of affording.

I have the honor to be your most obedient servant,

HENRY BERGH,

President.

The Committee cannot forbear to express their deep regret, at the opposition met with at Albany during the past session of the Legislature, and the defeat of the bill presented by the Society.

During the year the Society has lost by death several generous and distinguished friends. We have been called on to lament the decease of Mr. George T. Trimble, one of our Vice-Presidents, and Messrs. John D. Wolfe and Robert J. Dillon, of the Executive Committee.

The present ambulance of the Society being found to be insufficient, your Committee ordered a new one to be built possessing many improvements, at an expense of eight hundred and fifty dollars.

The Committee do not feel it necessary for them to refer to the general work of the Society, as the report of the Secretary furnishes it in detail.

THE NEW AMBULANCE.

Treasurer's Report.

— ◆•◆ —

THE Treasurer reports the income of the Society during the year ending 30th April, 1873, including the balance brought forward from the preceding year, was $33,130.43. This amount included the proceeds of the sale of $11,000 in U. S. bonds.

The expenditure during the same period was $27,-297.18.

This amount included a payment of twenty thousand two hundred and fifty dollars on account of the purchase of the new headquarters of the Society, leaving a balance of $5,833.25 in hand.

The society had also received by virtue of the real estate of the late Mr. Bonard, which was handed over to the Society in December last, $15,532.35.

It had expended from that amount $7,133.19, leaving a balance in hand of $8,399.16.

Total balance in hand 1st May, 1873, $14,232.41.

Liabilities same date $20,000, being the balance of purchase-money on headquarters.

Dr. The American Society for the Prevention of Cruelty to Animals, in account with Henry Clews, Treasurer. **Cr.**

1873.
May 1. *To Cash paid out from 1st May, 1872, to 30th April, 1873, inclusive, viz.:*

Salaries in office	$865 00
Salaries Special Agents	2,554 00
Rent of New York office and cleaning same	640 00
Rent of Brooklyn office	22 25
Rewards	212 25
Printing Annual Report, etc	356 20
Part purchase of house 100 East Twenty-second st	20,250 00
Purchase of gas fixtures for ditto	80 76
Stationery and books	143 19
Shields for Special Agents and State Societies	47 90
Rent of ambulance stable for the year	220 00
Set of new wheels, repairs, etc., to ambulance	145 55
Horse hire for ambulance	147 50
Painting and repairing hydrants	29 74
Telegrams, express charges, and sundries	32 98
Newspapers and pamphlets	83 25
Postage and revenue stamps	80 97
Stenographer's reports of counsel's arguments	85 10
Office furniture and fuel	61 11
Picture frames	45 00
Travelling expenses of Pres't and counsel to Albany, procuring legislation	605 87
Traveling expenses of Special Agents	233 06
Rents transferred to Estate Account	77 00
Donation to "Animal Kingdom" and cards for schools	98 50
Safe for office and removing same	165 00
Advertisements	15 00

Total expenditures		$27,297 18
Balance in Union Trust Company	$5,793 97	
In petty cash drawer	39 28	
		5,833 25
		$33,130 43

1872.
May 1. *By balance—*

Building fund	$9,550 00	
Current expenses	2,143 48	
		$11,693 48

1873.
May 1. *By Cash received from 1st May, 1872, to 30th April, 1873, inclusive, viz.:*

Donations	5,408 65
Legacy of Mrs. C. Johnstone	250 00
Yearly memberships	1,128 00
Fines received	1,202 86
Interest received on $9,000 U. S. 5-30 bonds and premium	306 80
Interest received on $2,000 U. S. 10-40 bonds and premiums	78 73
Interest on deposit from Union Trust Company	350 02
Proceeds of the sale of $9,000 U. S. 5-20 bonds	10,395 00
Proceeds of the sale of $2,000 U. S. 10-40 bonds	2,225 00
Rents of house in Madison St	77 00
Sale of sundry house fixture	12 00

	$33,130 43

ESTATE OF LOUIS BONARD.

1873.

May 1. *To Cash Paid Out.*

Taxes on Property............................	$1,685 10
A. H. Campbell, in settlement with him....	2,000 00
Repairs to Tenement Houses.................	113 09
Dr. M. Clymer, allowance as Medical Expert on Probate of Will......................	1,500 00
Dr. W. H. Hammond, allowance as Medical Expert on Probate of Will..............	1,500 00
Premiums on Insurances of Property.......	330 00
Sundries, paid A. Turner....................	5 00
	$7,133 19
Balance as per Bank Book....................	8,399 16
	$15,532 35

1873.

May 1. *By Cash Received.*

Cash received per W. A. Seaver, Receiver of the Estate..................................	$12,279 50
Rents received of Property, less Agent's Commission, etc.........................	3,252 85
	$15,532 35

REPORT OF AUDITING COMMITTEE.

NEW YORK, May 23, 1873.

We, the undersigned, have this day examined the general and the real estate accounts of the American Society for the Prevention of Cruelty to Animals, as exhibited to us by books and vouchers, and find that the same are correct, and in accordance therewith.

N. M. BECKWITH,
NATHAN C. ELY.

NOMINATIONS.

The report of the Committee on Nominations was then read :

Having been appointed a Committee on Nominations, we have fulfilled the duty imposed on us, and beg leave to recommend the following ticket for the suffrage of members.

W. B. DINSMORE,
C. L. TIFFANY,
DANIEL BUTTERFIELD,
} *Nominating Committee.*

May 7, 1873.

For President.
Henry Bergh.

For Vice-Presidents.

William H. Aspinwall,	John A. Dix,
Henry W. Bellows,	Benjamin D. Hicks,
James Brown,	John T. Hoffman,
Horace B. Claflin,	Marshall O. Roberts,
Peter Cooper.	Moses Taylor.

For Executive Committee.

Charles L. Anthony,	Charles Lanier,
N. M. Beckwith,	Frank Leslie,
John M. Bixby,	Charles H. Marshall,
Thomas C. Doremus,	Edward Matthews,
Nathan C. Ely,	Royal Phelps,
Eldridge T. Gerry.	James Stokes,
Townsend Harris,	Alfred Schermerhorn,

Alexander Van Rensselaer.

For Treasurer.
Henry Clews.

For Counsel.
Eldridge T. Gerry.

For Secretary.
N. P. Hosack.

For Veterinary Surgeons.

Charles C. Grice,	Alex. F. Liautard.

Messrs. Sinclair Tousey and Moses Solomons were appointed tellers, and the ballot resulted in the gentlemen recommended by the Committee on Nominations being unanimously elected.

T. W. HARTFIELD,

Acting Secretary.

After some interesting remarks from the Rev. Henry W. Bellows and Nathan C. Ely, Esq., upon the success which had attended the efforts of the Society, the former gentleman proposed the following resolution, which was seconded by Charles Lanier, Esq., and carried unanimously :

" That the President and Executive Committee of the American Society for the Prevention of Cruelty to Animals be, and they are hereby, authorized to ask from the public authorities an appropriation of $75,000, for the purpose of erecting five hundred or more drinking fountains in the City of New York, in accordance with a resolution passed some time since by the Common Council."

The presiding officer appointed Mr. Nathan C. Ely and N. M. Beckwith Auditing Committee.

A motion to adjourn was then made by Mr. Townsend Harris, and seconded by Mr. James Stokes, and carried, and the meeting adjourned accordingly.

OUR NEW HEADQUARTERS.

Since the organization of the Society in 1866, its limited funds have confined it to quarters totally inadequate to its necessities. As year after year passed, and the operations became more extended, the need of suitable offices became more urgent. Several attempts from

time to time were made by friends to raise sufficient
funds with which to erect a building for the occupancy
of the Society worthy of the humane cause in which it
was engaged; but up to the time of the death of the
late Mr. Louis Bonard, the Building Fund had not
reached ten thousand dollars. The munificent bequest
of that benevolent gentleman placed the Society on a
more solid footing, and to-day it stands possessed of an
elegant building as its new headquarters. It is situated
on the corner of Fourth Avenue and Twenty-second
street, and is built of brown stone and brick. It is a
four-story English basement house, and was purchased
by the Society for forty thousand dollars. The ambulances
are contained within it; and in point of convenience and
elegance, it is doubtless the finest edifice owned or employed in the cause of brute protection.

HUMANE DISPOSAL OF VAGRANT DOGS.

The following communication on this subject was addressed to the Mayor, and by him referred to the Board
of Alderman; which body, after indulging in much unbecoming levity, rejected the proffered services of the
Society.

AMERICAN SOCIETY FOR THE PREVENTION
OF CRUELTY TO ANIMALS,
April 5, 1873.

To HIS HONOR W. F. HAVEMEYER.

DEAR SIR: The season being near when it is supposed that dogs are
most inclined to become rabid, it seems appropriate to take some action in
the matter. With this regard I venture to offer the following suggestions,
to wit: That the City appropriate a lot of ground somewhere on this
island, and erect a small building in the center thereof, to be used for the
temporary confinement and destruction of these animals by the employment of carbonic acid gas, a speedy, merciful and noiseless process. This
building, which need be of inconsiderable cost, should be provided with
lodgings for the custodian and his family, and, above the four sides of the
wall or fence which incloses the lot, separate kennels to be provided,
wherein the dogs may be confined pending their recognition and removal

by their owners, or failit g in this, when valueless, their destruction. To effect the removal from the street of these friendless and vagrant creatures, I propose that men go about the City early in the morning, followed either by our ambulance or a special vehicle for that purpose, and that the dogs be captured by the aid of scoop nets, and then carried to their place of destination for final disposal. I think your Honor will not fail to perceive the superiority of this mode of disposing of this difficulty over the cruel, demoralizing and imperfect means formerly employed by this City. Nor, as experience has shown, does the giving of rewards for their delivery at a pound accomplish the object in view; but, on the contrary, augments the difficulty by increasing their number in proportion to the premium offered. Through the humane interposition of this Society, these rewards having ceased for several years, it is obvious the number of vagrant dogs in the streets has greatly diminished. Apart from the apprehension which many citizens feel on this subject, it is undeniable that the mute and suffering appeals of this friendly creature, so intimately allie l to our, race, are a source of a painful regret to every kind-hearted beholder. This Society, which in order to insure a merciful death when necessary, now destroys nearly all the disabled horses of this city and elsewhere in this State, would willingly undertake to do the same for the dogs, and take entire charge of the work, free of all remuneration, if the city government on its part would provide the premises and reimburse the Society its actual expenses in employes, an inconsiderable cost. Will your Honor please favor me with your views on this subject, or, in case you should approve of it, lay it before the Common Council, with your recommendations.

I have the honor to be yours, etc.,

HENRY BERGH,

President

TRANSPORTATION OF CATTLE.

The following laws for preventing cruelty to animals while in transit on railroads, have been enacted by Congress during the session just ended:

AN ACT to prevent cruelty to animals while in transit by railroad or other means of transportation within the United States.

Be it enacted by the Senate and House of Representatives of the United States of America in Congress assembled, That no railroad company within the United States whose road forms any part of a line of road over which cattle, sheep, swine, or other animals, shall be conveyed from one State to another, or the owners or masters of steam, sailing or other vessels carrying or transporting cattle, sheep, swine, or other animals, from one State to another, shall confine the same in cars, boats, or vessels of any description for a longer period than twenty-eight consecutive hours, without unloading the same for rest, water and feeding, for a period of at least five consecutive hours, unless prevented from so unloading by storm or other accidental causes. In estimating such confinement, the time during which the animals have been confined without such rest on connecting roads from which they are received shall be included, it being the intent of this act to prohibit their continuous confinement beyond the period of twenty-eight hours, except upon contingencies hereinbefore stated. Animals so unloaded shall be properly fed and watered during such rest, by the owner or person having the custody thereof, or in case of his default in so doing, then by the railroad company or owners or masters of boats or vessels transporting the same, at the expense of said owner or person in custody thereof; and said company, owners or masters shall in such cases, have a lien upon such animals for food, care and custody furnished, and shall not be liable for any detention of such animals authorized by this act. Any company, owner or custodian of such animals who shall knowingly and wilfully fail to comply with the provisions of this act shall, for each and every such failure to comply with the provisions of the act, be liable for and forfeit and pay a penalty of not less than one hundred nor more than five hundred dollars: *Provided, however,* That when animals shall be carried in cars, boats, or other vessels in which they can and do have proper food, water, space and opportunity for rest, the foregoing provisions in regard to their being unloaded shall not apply.

SEC. 2. That the penalty created by the first section of this act shall be recovered by civil action in the name of the United States, in the Circuit or District Court of the United States holden within the district where the violation of this act may have been committed, or the person or corporation resides or carries on its business; and it shall be the duty of all United States marshals, their deputies and subordinates, to prosecute all violations of this act which shall come to their notice or knowledge.

SEC. 3. That any person or corporation entitled to lien under the first section of this act may enforce the same by a petition filed in the District Court of the United States holden within the district where the food, care and custody shall have been furnished, or the owner or custodian of the property resides; and said court shall have power to issue all suitable process for the enforcement of such lien by sale or otherwise, and to compel the payment of all costs, penalties, charges, and expenses of proceedings under this act.

SEC. 4. That this act shall not go into effect until the first day of October, eighteen hundred and seventy-three.

SALTING THE STREETS.

This abominable practice on the part of railroad and omnibus proprietors is still continued, and never to as great an extent as during the past winter, by which thousands of horses have been ruined and the public health impaired. A stringent City ordinance exists prohibiting this dangerous custom; but it has been allowed to become obsolete. An effort was made by the Society to effect the passage of a law by the Legislature this session designed to prevent its recurrence; but, although petitions, signed by thousands of horse owners of New York and Brooklyn, were presented asking for its enactment, it was killed through the influence of the above-named arbitrary corporations.

The following sketches illustrate the destructive results to the feet of horses:

No. 1.

No. 1 shows the natural hoof, with a dotted line marking the "slush line," to which the hoof sinks in the mire.

No. 2

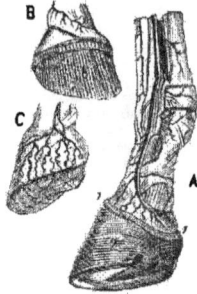

No. 2.—A shows the anatomical appearance of the fetlock and hoof. 1 in A shows the upper part of the sensitive lamina, and 2 the horny part.

B, in No. 2, shows the hoof after the horny part is removed; b, within, shows the sensitive lamina, which fits close to the hoof, and looks like the inside of a toadstool.

C, in No. 2, shows the bony part of the hoof, without the cover of the sensitive lamina.

39

No. 3.

No. 3 shows the ulceration beginning on the upper part of the hoof.

No. 4.

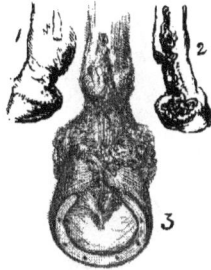

No. 4 indicates different specimens of the diseased hoofs in the early stages of the ulceration.

No. 5

No. 5 shows the terrible ravages made by the ulcerations in a hoof which has been diseased for a little time.

No. 6.

1

2

THE GYRO PIGEON.

A most ingenious substitute in pigeon matches for the live bird has been invented and offered for sale by the agents, Messrs. Schuyler, Hartley & Graham, 20 John street, New York. The apparatus consists of a finely tempered steel counterfeit pigeon and a trap. An inclosed spring being wound up, the direction set, the gyro placed on two steel points above the spring, and at the signal pulled ; the gyro immediately ascends, going in the desired direction. Sometimes the counterfeit bird will pass near the ground ; at others, describe an extensive elevated curve, and at others unite all the eccentric motions of a live pigeon. Every desired feature of pigeon shooting is attained by this means, without being guilty of wantonly butchering a sentient being. The gyro has on several occasions been tested by the officers of this Society, and highly approved of The accompanying illustrations are from *Frank Leslie'. Illustrated Paper.*

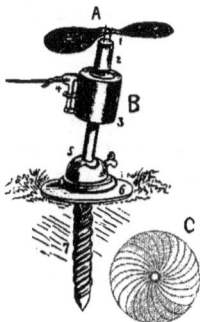

"THE ANIMAL KINGDOM."

With the beginning of the present year appeared the first number of THE ANIMAL KINGDOM, a journal devoted to the interests of this Society, and edited by Mr. Geo. W. Johnston. The paper, the first of its kind ever published in this State, has already met with a warm welcome from the friends of the cause. In an educational point of view this periodical can hardly be over-estimated, and it will prove a valuable accessory to the Society. Short stories, sketches, and other interesting miscellaneous matter pertinent to the character of the paper, will be found in its columns, all tending to render it a moral and refining family journal.

The subscription price of THE ANIMAL KINGDOM is one dollar a year. Those who desire to take the paper, can send their subscriptions to this office, or to the office of publication, 210 E. 13th street, addressed to the editor.

TESTIMONIAL TO MR. GERRY.

THE Society has presented to its Counsel, Mr. Elbridge T. Gerry, a silver vase, of which an illustration appears herewith. It is of massive silver, standing 18 inches high, and exquisitely designed and executed. Upon the sides of the pedestal, not appropriated to the inscription, are beautiful bas reliefs, one showing the shield of the Society, another a group of horned animals, and the third, touchingly illustrates, the fidelity and love of the dog, sleeping on the grave of its master. The inhabitants of the sea, as well as of earth and air are also happily represented, and the structure, resting as it does, upon the backs of turtles, is suggestive of one of the earilest, efforts of the Society in its labors of reform. The following is the correspondence resulting from its pre-sentation:

AMERICAN SOCIETY FOR THE PREVENTION OF CRUELTY TO ANIMALS.

HEAD QUARTERS FOURTH AVENUE, CORNER OF 22D ST. }
NEW YORK, June 15, 1873. }

Elbridge T. Gerry Esq.:

DEAR SIR: At a meeting of the Executive Committee of this Society, the following resolution was offered and unanimously adopted:

"That the President be authorized to cause a suitable testimonial to be made, expressive of the grateful recognition on the part of this Society of the able and meritorious professional services of Mr. Elbridge T. Gerry, in the cause to which it is devoted."

In the performance of this agreeable duty, I have endeavored, while carrying out the views of the committee, to illustrate through the medium of a silver vase the chronology and purposes of the Society. One of its earliest efforts, as you may remember, was directed to the amelioration of the treatment of a creature, popularly regarded as one of the lowest in the order of animated nature, but which the learned Agassiz has declared to be among the most sensitive of animals, namely, the turtle.

Hence upon the backs of four of this race of beings the superstructure rests, as on a foundation. Upon a quadrilateral pedestal are seen, in bas-relief and otherwise, the several representative orders as classified by zoology; and as a crowning glory to the work, that paragon of animals, the horse, is shown in high artistic beauty on the basin.

While thus attempting a brief description of the token offered, the committee would not withhold its commendation of the taste and skill which the house of Messrs. Tiffany & Co. have manifested in the execution of it. There but remains for me to ask you, in the name of the Society I represent, to accept it as an expression of its appreciation of your eminent attainments and devotion to the humane and civilizing labor it has in charge. I have the honor to be yours,

HENRY BERGH, *President.*

Henry Bergh Esq., President:

DEAR SIR: The slight professional aid I may have hitherto rendered this Society was to me a matter of pleasure rather than of duty. The cause embodied in it, and impersonated by yourself, so commends itself to every right-thinking person in the community that its own humanity

has always been its strongest plea. The numerous decisions in its favor
in the legal tribunals are simply the result of just applications of law in
response to its claims for mercy to the defenseless brute. Indeed, they
seem to illustrate the uprightness of the judiciary rather than the ability
of the counsel, for the weakest advocate becomes necessarily able when
pleading for a cause so just and righteous. The superb gift of the Society
I shall ever prize and value. Its design, which so admirably illustrates
the work of the institution, is a speaking tribute to the artistic mind which
planned it, while its execution is certainly a marvel of art and beauty.
I beg you will convey to the Executive Committee of the Society my full
appreciation of this elegant compliment, and of their very flattering
resolution which accompanied it.

With great respect, etc.,

ELBRIDGE T. GERRY.

New York, June 16, 1873.

Societies in the United States and Canada.

Organized and Originated after the example of the American Society for the Prevention of Cruelty to Animals at New York.

NEW YORK.

American Society for the Prevention of Cruelty to Animals.

Organized in New York City, 1866.

HENRY BERGH, Pres.   HENRY CLEWS, Treas.
E. T. GERRY, Counsel.   N. P. HOSACK, Sec.
T. W. HARTFIELD, Superintendent.

BRANCHES

OF THE AMERICAN SOCIETY FOR THE PREVENTION OF CRUELTY TO ANIMALS IN THE STATE OF NEW YORK.

ALBANY BRANCH.

Organized February, 1869.

ROBERT LENNOX BANKS,   JOHN M. CRAPO,
        President.   1st Vice-President.
A. K. RICHARDS, Treasurer.

BUFFALO BRANCH.

Organized April 4, 1867.

SILAS KINGSLEY, President.   DANIEL D. NASH, Secretary.
HENRY HOWARD, Treasurer.

WOMEN'S BRANCH, BUFFALO.

Organized, 1871.

Mrs. H. SEYMOUR, President. | Mrs. J. C. LORD, Vice-President
Mrs. I. H. YERKES, Secretary. | Miss L. LORD, 2d Vice-President
Miss H. L. HAYES, Treasurer.

FISHKILL BRANCH, FISHKILL, N. Y.

Organized August, 1869.

J. HOWLAND, President. J. HERVEY COOK, Secretary.
HORATIO N. SWIFT, Treasurer.

FLUSHING BRANCH.

Organized, 1872.

ISAAC BLOODGOOD, President. | BENJ. W. DOWNING, Secretary

LADIES' AUXILIARY BRANCH, FLUSHING.

Mrs. MARY PELL, President. | Mrs. C. MYER, Vice-President.
Mrs. I. C. HICKS, Secretary. | Mrs. C. HUNTSMAN, "
Mrs. E. H. PARSONS, Treasurer. | Miss A. L. HICKS, "

KINGSTON.

List of Officers not received.

AUBURN.

List of Officers not received.

POUGHKEEPSIE BRANCH.

H. L. YOUNG, President. | O. D. M. BAKER, Cor. Sec'y.
HENRY V. PELTON, Rec. Sec'y. | H. C. SMITH, Treasurer.

SING SING BRANCH.

Organized, 1872.

ISAAC B. NOXON, President | AARON YOUNG, Vice-President.
Z. C. INSLEE, Secretary. | S. M. SHERWOOD, Treasurer.
Miss DUSENBERRY, Cor. Secretary.

CONNECTICUT.

Society for the Prevention of Cruelty to Animals.

Organized at Hartford, 1873.

R. S. ELY, President.
HON. G. A. FAY,
    2d Vice-President.

HON. E. H. HYDE, 1st Vice-Pres.
HON. H. C. BECKWITH,
    3d Vice-President

CALIFORNIA.

San Francisco Society for the Prevention of Cruelty to Animals.

Organized, 1871.

HENRY GIBBONS, M.D., Pres't.
JACOB Z. DAVIS, Vice-President.

JAS. S. HUTCHINSON, Treas.
N. HUNTER, Recording Sec'y.

JOS. A. WOODSON, Corresponding Secretary.

PETALUMA, CAL.

Society for the Prevention of Cruelty to Animals.

Organized at Petaluma.

J. SNOW ....Secretary.

CANADA.

Metropolitan Society for the Prevention of Cruelty to Animals.

Organized at Ottawa, 1871.

E. MARTINEAU,
    President.

H. J. M'LARDY,
    Secretary and Treasurer.

MONTREAL.

The Canadian Society for the Prevention of Cruelty to Animals.

Organized at Montreal, 1869.

WILLIAM WORKMAN,
    President.

F. MACKENZIE,
    Secretary and Treasurer.

48

Ladies' Humane Education Committee of above Society:

MRS. ANDREW ALLAN,
President. | MRS. G. W. SIMPSON,
Vice-President.

MISS A. McCORD, Secretary and Treasurer.

QUEBEC.

Quebec Society for the Prevention of Cruelty to Animals.

Organized, 1870.

ROBERT HAMILTON, President. | W. J. MACADAMS, Secretary.
W. HOSSACK, Treasurer.

COLORADO TERRITORY.

Colorado Society for the Prevention of Cruelty to Animals.

Organized at Denver, 1872.

DAVID A. CHEVER, President.   HYATT HUSSEY, Treasurer.
WILBUR C. LOTHROP, Secretary.

DISTRICT OF COLUMBIA.

WASHINGTON, D. C.

Organized April, 1870.

THEODORE F. GATCHEL, Pres. | A. S. SOLOMONS, Treasurer.

GEORGIA.

Organized at Augusta, 1873.

JAMES W. DAVIES, Pres.   SAMUEL DUTCHER, Sec and Counsel.
B. BENSON, Treasurer.

ILLINOIS.

Illinois Humane Society.

Organized at Chicago, 1871.

EDWIN L. BROWN, President | W. H. SHARP, Secretary.
SAMUEL T. ATWATER, Treasurer.

IOWA.

Scott County Society for the Prevention of Cruelty to
Animals.

R. McINTOSH, President. | G. E. HUBBELL, Secretary.

INDIANA.

INDIANAPOLIS.

(Ordinances to prevent Cruelty to Animals passed December, 1863.)

KENTUCKY.

Kentucky Society for the Prevention of Cruelty to Animals.

Organized at Louisville, 1873.

B. F. AVERY, President | W. C. KENNEDY, Treasurer.
W. F. REYNOLDS, JR., Secretary.

MASSACHUSETTS.

Organized at Boston.

Massachusetts Society for the Prevention of Cruelty to
Animals.

GEORGE T. ANGELL, President. | FRANK B. FAY, Secretary.
HENRY SALTONSTALL, Treasurer.

BRANCHES OF THE MASSACHUSETTS SOCIETY.

Taunton (Mass.) Humane Society.

Organized, 1871.

SAMUEL L. CROCKER, Pres. | WILLIAM MASON, Vice-Pres.

Executive Committee.

SAMUEL L. CROCKER,   EDMUND W. PORTER,
DANIEL L. MITCHELL,   JOHN H. CHURCH
GEORGE M. HAMLEN, Sec.   NATHAN H. SKINNER, Treas.

Newburyport (Mass.) and Vicinity Society.

Organized, 1871.

E. S. MOSELEY, President.   G. W. CLARK, Treasurer.
Thirty Vice-Presidents.   City Marshal for the time being,
JOSEPH MAY, Secretary.   Agent.

Haverhill (Mass.) Society.

Organized, 1871.

REV. W. H. SPENCER, President. | MRS. G. W. GEARY, Secretary.
C. D. HUNKING, Treasurer.

MAINE.

Bangor Society for the Prevention of Cruelty to Animals.

J. D. WARREN, President. | T. G. STICKNEY, Treasurer.
O. H. INGALLS, Secretary.

Portland (Me.) Society for the Prevention of Cruelty to Animals.

Organized, 1872.

WOODBURY S. DANA, Pres.   JOSEPH W. SYMONDS, Treas.
STANLEY T. PULLEN, Sec.   MRS. L. D. M. SWEAT, Cor. Sec.

MARYLAND.

Maryland Society for the Prevention of Cruelty to Animals·

Organized at Baltimore, 1869.

WILLIAM WOODWARD, Pres. | T. H. BELT JR., Secretary.
JOSEPH GEEGAN, JR., Treasurer.

MINNESOTA.

Minnesota Society for the Prevention of Cruelty to Animals.

Organized at St. Paul, March, 1870.

F. DE COU, ESQ., President. | W. R. MARSHALL, Vice-President.
E. W. CHASE, Secretary. | W. L. WILSON, Treasurer.

MICHIGAN.

Michigan Society for the Prevention of Cruelty to Animals.

Organized at Detroit, 1870.

GOVERNOR H. P. BALDWIN, President. | DAVID PRESTON, Treasurer.
MOSES W. FIELD, Cor. Sec.
E. W. MEDDAUGH, Rec. Secretary.

MISSOURI.

Humane Society of Missouri.

Organized at St. Louis, 1870.

HON. GEORGE PARTRIDGE, President. | W. H. MAURICE. Treasurer.
P. G. FERGUSON, Secretary.

NEW JERSEY.

New Jersey Society for the Prevention of Cruelty to Animals.

Organized at Newark, April 21, 1869.

MOSES BIGELOW. President. | AARON M. RING, Treasurer.
R. WATSON GILDER. Secretary. | F. W. LEONARD, Attorney.

JERSEY CITY.

Hudson County Society for the Prevention of Cruelty to
Animals.

J. J. YOULIN, M. 'D., President. | S. H. SMITH, Vice-President.
W. H. MUIRHEAD, Secretary. | DANIEL McLEOD, Treasurer.
C. S. SEE, Assistant Sec. | J. F. McGEE, Counsel.

TRENTON, NEW JERSEY.

Society for the Prevention of Cruelty to Animals.

Organized, 1873.

REV. J. C. BROWN, President. | EZRA B. FULLER, Treasurer.
LEWIS PARKER, JR., Sec. | F. KINGMAN, Counsel.

PATERSON, NEW JERSEY.

Passaic County Society for the Prevention of Cruelty to
Animals.

Organized, 1873.

REV. F. BANVARD, President.

NEW HAMPSHIRE.

Society for the Prevention of Cruelty to Animals.

Organized at Portsmouth, 1872.

ALBERT R. HATCH, President. | A. P. STEVENS, Secretary.

BOYS' SOCIETY, PORTSMOUTH, N. H.

Organized December, 1872.

J. B. TIFFANY, President. | F. G. BUSH, and P. LAMPREY,
W. MOORE, Recording Sec. | Vice-Presidents.
H. B. KENT, Cor. Sec. | W. F. STEARNS, Treasurer.

NORTH CAROLINA.

Society for the Prevention of Cruelty to Animals.

Organized at Newberne, 1871.

GEORGE C. RIXFORD, Pres. | ROBERT C. KEHOE, Treasurer.
JULIUS ASH, Recording Sec'y. | GEORGE W. NASON, Cor. Sec.

OHIO.

Society for the Prevention of Cruelty to Animals.

Organized at Toledo, 1871.

A. T. STEBBINS, President. | JOHN KAUFMANN, Treasurer.
RALPH H. WAGGONER, Secretary.

CLEVELAND, OHIO.

Society for the Prevention of Cruelty to Animals.

Organized, 1873.

(List of Officers not Received.)

CINCINNATI, OHIO.

(Society now being Organized.)

COLUMBUS, OHIO.

(Society about being Organized.)

OREGON.

Society for the Prevention of Cruelty to Animals.

Organized at Portland, 1872.

W. T. SHANAHAN, Secretary.

(Laws now under consideration by the Legislature.)

54

PENNSYLVANIA.

Pennsylvania Society for the Prevention of Cruelty to Animals.

Dr. A. L. ELWYN, President. | P. E. CHASE, Secretary.
ROB'T R. CORSON, Treasurer.

Ladies' Pennsylvania Society for the Prevention of Cruelty to Animals.

Mrs. CAROLINE E. WHITE, President. | Miss S. L. BALDWIN, Cor. Secretary.
Miss ELIZABETH MORhIS, Rec. Secretary. | Miss JACOBS, Treasurer.

LANCASTER, PENN.

Society for the Prevention of Cruelty to Animals.

Organized at Lancaster, 1872.

JOHN B. WARFEL, President. | G. W. REICHENBACH, Sec.
AMOS S. HENDERSON, Treasurer.

YORK CO., (PENN.) SOCIETY.

Organized Nov. 28, 1872.

Rev. WM. BAUM, D. D., Pres. | J. C. LUITWIELER, Secretary.

RHODE ISLAND.

PROVIDENCE.

Society for the Prevention of Cruelty to Animals.

Hon. G. L. CLARKE, President. | N. A FISHER,
JOHN W. ANGELL, Treasurer. | General Agent and Sec'y.
WILLIAM LLOYD BOWERS, Prosecuting Agent.

LADIES' AUXILIARY SOCIETY, PROVIDENCE.

Organized Jan., 1872.

MRS. WM. A ROBINSON, President.	MRS. ALBERT DAILEY, MRS. SYLVESTER TAYLOR, Vice-Presidents.
MRS. STEPHEN ATWATER, Secretary.	MISS MARY A. ROBINSON, Treas.

TEXAS.

The Galveston Agricultural, Horticultural and Industrial Association.

Organized July, 1871.

Is empowered by the Legislature of the State, to prevent Cruelty to domestic and other Animals, and its officers and members are authorized to arrest offenders and bring them before the courts of law.

PHILIP C. TUCKER, President.	N. B. YARD. Treasurer.
M. HOBBY, Actuary.	WM. T. AUSTIN, Sr., Secretary.

TENNESSEE.

Society for the Prevention of Cruelty to Animals.

Organized at Nashville, 1871.

(List of Officers not received.)

VIRGINIA.

Society for the Prevention of Cruelty to Animals.

WATERFORD.

W. WILLIAMS, President.	COL. S. E. CHAMBERLAIN, Treas.
PROF. E. H. WALKER, Secretary.	

WEST VIRGINIA.

Society for the Prevention of Cruelty to Animals in course of organization at Charleston.

AGENTS.

List of Agents of the American Society for the Prevention of Cruelty to Animals in the State of New York.

ANDREWS, S. N......................Little Falls, Herkimer Co.
ALLIS, A. G........................Syracuse, Onondaga Co.
AVERY, WILLIAM...................Highland Falls, Orange Co.
BEVINS, S. H.......................Bollon, Warren Co.
BLAKE, CHARLES..................Hudson, Columbia Co.
BOYD, S...........................New Rochelle, W'chester Co.
BUCKLEY, WADE..................Port Jervis, Orange Co.
BRITTON, ALONZO..................Rochester, Monroe Co.
BARRETT, E. G....................Bedford Station, W'chester Co.
BROWN, WILLIAM..................Rochester, N. Y.
CAW, D. J.........................Schenectady, Sch'tady Co.
CHAPIN, G. B.....................Ogdensburg, St. L'rence Co.
CHUMASEN, J. C..................Rochester, Monroe Co.
CLAY, HALL H....................Little Falls, Herkimer Co.
CORNELL, H. K...................Greenwich, Washington Co.
CROWLEY, F......................Tompkinsville, Richmond Co.
CARLEY, J. G....................Schenectady, Schenectady Co.
FISKE, E. B......................Perry, Wyoming Co.
FOWLER, NEHEMIAH.............Newburgh, Orange Co.
FLINT, CLEMENT, M. D.........Sand Lake, N. Y.
GRIFFITH, L. E.................Troy, Rensselaer Co.
GILBERT, DANIEL...............Saratoga Springs, Saratoga Co.
HARRISON, R. F................Canton, St. Lawrence Co.
HINRICHS, J....................Jamaica, Queens Co.
HILDRETH, J. F................Brooklyn, Kings Co.
JONES, W. F....................Cohoes, Albany Co.
KEMBLE, GEORGE...............Grove St., N. Y. City.
KINNEY, JAMES................Brooklyn, Kings Co.
LAWRENCE, ALFRED............Tarrytown, W'chester Co.
LATHROP, J.....................Kinderhook, Columbia Co.
LEWIS, WILLIAM................Astoria, Queens Co.
MILLER, A. J...................Brewster Station, Putnam Co.
MILLER, JOHN..................East New York, Kings Co.
MILLER, J. DEWITT............Fort Edward, Washington Co.
MORTIMER, C. J...............33 Barclay St. N. Y. City.
NOTEWARE, NORMAN W.........Chappaqua, Westchester Co.
O'BRIEN, JAMES...............Kingston, Ulster Co.
PARKHURST, I. F..............Bath, Steuben Co.

POTTER, JOHN F ....Greenw'h IronW'ks,OrangeCo.
PHILIPS.A. J......... ....Brooklyn, Kings Co.
PILSON, GEORGE.............. ......Yonkers, Westchester Co.
RUTSER, W. H......................31 Cortlandt St , N. Y. City.
RICH, ALDEMAH W.................Valley Stream, Queens Co.
SMITH, WALTER Mc................Jamaica. Queens Co.
SMITH, D. C..................... ....Brooklyn, Kings Co.
STEPHENS, D. B....................White Plains, Westchester Co.
SNEDEN, R. K.........................Spring Valley, Rockland Co.
SMITH, H. W.........................Castile, Wyoming Co.
STACY, GEORGE.....................Nanuet, Rockland Co.
STEVENS, A. L......................Troy, Rensselaer Co.
SPENCER, JOSHUA O...............Westchester Co.
TAYLOR, H. A..'............ ......Malone, Franklin Co.
TOELL, JOHN.....................New Lots, Kings Co.
TILLINGHAST, JOHN ....Utica, Oneida Co.
TOLTON, I. C................ ....Cold Springs, Suffolk Co.
VAN VOLKINLIGH. C. M.............Kinderhook, Columbia Co.
WOOLSEY, C. MEECH..............Milton. Ulster Co.
WHEELER, LAWRENCE W.........Washington av., Morrisania.

— •◆•——

DONATIONS OF BOOKS, PAMPHLETS AND NEWS-PAPERS.

New York Sunday Dispatch.
New York Round Table and Citizen.
Wilkes' Spirit of the Times.
Frank Leslie's Illustrated Weekly.
Scottish American.
The Nation.
The Daily Brooklyn Union.
The Daily Brooklyn Times.
The Home Journal.
The Turf, Field and Farm.
The Anglo-American.
The Christian Weekly.
Webster's Elegant Illustrated Dictionary, 1871. Donated by the Publishers, Messrs. G. & C. Merriam, of Springfield, Mass., to the President.

Laws of New York State, 1867, 1868, 1869. 6 vols. Donated by H. Nelson, Esq., Secretary of State of New York State.

Agricultural Reports, 1867, 1868. Donated by H. Capron, Esq., Commissioner of Agriculture, Washington, D. C.

Report of the Iowa Agricultural Society, 1867. Donated by J. M. Schaffer, Secretary of the Society.

Report of the Pennsylvania Society, Philadelphia.

Laws of the Geneva Society for the Prevention of Cruelty to Animals.

Report of the Canadian Society for

Report of Texas Cattle Disease. Donated by Dr. E. Harris.

Report of the Society for the Prevention of Cruelty to Animals at the Hague, Holland.

Report of the Metropolitan Board of Health, 1868. Presented by the Board.

Bulletins de la Societe Protectrice des Animaux. Paris Mai, 1869, to Mai, 1871.

Bulletins de la Societe Protectrice des Animaux. Bruxelles, Mai 1869, to Mai, 1871.

Report of the Board of Commissioners of Central Park, 1868. Donated by the Board.

Report of the Scottish Society for 1870.

The Animal World, a monthly magazine, published by the Royal Society for the Prevention of Cruelty to Animals, London.

Manual of the Corporation of the City of New York. Donated by John Shannon, Esq., Clerk Common Council.

Reports of the New York State Agricultural Society for 1867, 1868. Donated by the Society.

Sanitary Code of the Board of Health, 1870.

Practical Horseshoeing, by G. Fleming, F. R. G. S. Donated by the Scottish Society for the Prevention of Cruelty to Animals.

Report of the Glasgow Scottish Society for 1871.

Report of the Woman's Branch of the Pennsylvania Society, Philadelphia.

Post-office Directory. Donated by the U. S. Post-office Department.

Our Dumb Animals. Published monthly by the Massachusetts Society for the Prevention of Cruelty to Animals. Boston.

The Advertiser's Hand-Book. Donated by Messrs. Pettengill & Co.

The Animal's Friend. Published by some members of the San Francisco Society for the Prevention of Cruelty to Animals.

Report of the Board of Health. New York, 1871.

Kentucky Society for the Prevention of Cruelty to Animals. Annual Report for 1873.

Ohio—Laws of the State of. Presented by W. A. Knapp, Adjutant General of the State.

Statutory Crimes—Bishop on. Presented by Geo. T. Angell, Esq., Boston.

Striking for the Right. Presented by the Authoress, Miss Julia A. Eastman.

Reports of the Proceedings of various Foreign Societies.

To those who may feel disposed to donate, by WILL, to
the benevolent objects of this Society, the following is submitted as a form :

FORM OF BEQUEST OF PERSONAL PROPERTY.

I give and bequeath unto "The American Society for
the Prevention of Cruelty to Animals," a corporation
created by, and existing under the laws of the State of
New York, the sum of......................dollars,
to be applied to the uses of said corporation.

FORM OF DEVISE OF REAL PROPERTY.

I give and devise unto "The American Society for
the Prevention of Cruelty to Animals," a corporation
created by, and existing under the laws of the State of
New York, all (here insert description of property)
Together with all the appurtenances, tenements and
hereditaments thereunto belonging or in anywise apper-
taining. To have and to hold the same unto the said
corporation, its successors and assigns, forever.

LIST OF MEMBERS.

THOSE MARKED * ARE LIFE MEMBERS.

Adams, Miss E., M. D.
Assing, Miss O.
*Aspinwall, William H.
Acton, Thos. C.
Ames, Angelo
*Appleton, D. S.
Aspinwall, Lloyd
American News Co.
*Anthony & Hall
Adams, Mrs. A. O.
Astoin, F.
*Arnold, Constable & Co.
Alvord, Mrs. C. F.

Bedell, T.
Bennett, L.
Barlow, Mrs. F. C.
Bell, Miss K.
Bissell, Wm. H., M. D.
Bartlett, Edw. G., M. D.
Buckley, Wade
Bathgate, Chas. W.
Beckwith, N. M.
Beers, Edwin
Bliss, Archibald M.
*Brown, Stewart

Blakslee, H. A.
*Brown, James
Brooks, Erastus
Bellows, Rev. Henry W.
Bryant, William C.
*Belmont, August
Bristed, C. Astor
*Bergh, Henry
*Bixby, John M.
Berghaus, Albert
*Booth, Edwin
*Ball, Black & Co.
*Babcock, Bros. & Co.
Brown, Mrs. Addison
*Bonner, Robert
*Barney, D. N.
Buchanan, Perkins & Co
Blodget, Charles F.
Barnard, John T., Jr.
Bell, Mrs. George
Bedell, C. V.

Cooper, Peter
Cisco, John J.
*Clews, Henry
*Claflin, Horace B.
Cameron, S. F.
Collins, Mrs. C. E.
Curtis, Mrs. G. W.
Curtis, Miss E. B.
Clapp, Mrs.
Carr, Walter
*Colby, Gardner R.
*Chittenden, S. B. & Co.
Cary, William F.
*Crapo, John M.
*Corse, Israel
Corwin, W. E.
Cocheu, F.
Conkling, F. A.
Coles, Mrs. B. G.
Clift, Smith
Campbell, John

Coggeshall, Edwin W.
Culver, E. D.

*Davis, O. Wilson
Dix, John A.
Dilks, George W.
*Duncan, W. Butler
*Dinsmore, W. B.
*Dolan, Miss Ellen
Dejonge, Louis
*Delmonico, Lorenzo
*Darling, Griswold & Co.
Doremus, Thomas C.
Dodge, Wm. E.
Dodge, Wm. E., Jr.
Deitz, Samuel

*Ely, Nathan C.
Ewen, John
Ewen, Miss Caroline
Ehrhardt, L. H. G., M. D.
Exton, Miss

*Fish, Hamilton
Fargo, William G.
Francis, S. W., M. D.
Farrell, John
*Faile, Thomas H.
French, Richard
Fairbanks, Mrs.
Frost, Miss E. R.
Frothingham, H.

*Griswold, George
*Gilbert, F. E.
*Greer, Turner & Co.
*Garrison & Allen
*Garner & Co.
*Groesbeck, David & Co.
*Green, John C.
*Gray, Horace
Grote, A. H.
*Gifford, Mrs. Ellen M.
*Gerry, Elbridge T.

Grote, Frederick

Harvey, Henry
Hudson, F. A.
Hoffman, John T.
Hall, A. Oakey
*Hicks, B. D.
*Hicks, Mrs. E. T.
Hoey, John
Hudson, E. D., M. D.
*Holland, Alexander
Howland, Meredith
*Hodgkins, Thomas G.
Herring, Silas C.
*Hoyts, Sprague & Co.
Hosack, N. P.
Hallgarten & Co.
*Hoe, R. & Co.
Harris, Townsend
Harrison, Mrs. Mary
*Hadden, John A.
Hoagland, J. S.
Hackley, Mrs.
Hewett, H. B.
Henriques, C. A.
Hoffman, Dr.
Herring, S. C.

*Ingersoll, Mrs. J. H.

*Jones, John D.
*Jaffray, E. S.
Johnson, Rowland
*Johnston, John Taylor
*Johnston, J. Boorman
*Jenkins & Vail
*Jackson, G. R., Burnet & Co.
*Jessup, Morris K.
Jaffe, Otto
Jackson, James

Knapp, Shepherd
*Kendall, Opdyke & Co.

Knower, John
Kettell, E. H.
Kapff, S. Ludwig
Kelso, J. I.

Lowell, Miss C. K.
Lowell Mrs. C. R.
Longman, R.
Leslie, Leon
*Lenox, James
*Leslie, Frank
*Lyle, John S.
*Lord, John T,
Ludlow, Edward H.
*Law, George
Low, Josah O.
*Lockwood, Le Grand
*Langley, W. C. & Co.
*Lea, J. & J. T. & Co.
*Low, Harriman & Co.
*Lanier, J. F. D.
Lanier, Charles
Loeffler, A.
Leslie, Henry
Leslie, Alfred
Livingston, Miss Annie L.
*Liautard, A., M. D.
Low, J. O.
Low, A. A.
Lowndes, William J.

*Murray, John B.
Morgan, Homer
Mortimer, Richard.
Menike, Mrs. Julia
*Moller, Wm. & Sons
*Mudge, E. R.,Sawyer & Co.
*McLean, George W.
Morris, Charles D.
*Marshall Charles H.
Martin, Richard
*Matthews, Edward
Merritt, Anna
Morris, Fordham

Macy, Josiah H.
Morris, Lewis G.
McKinley, James.
Mitchell, Samuel
*Moulton, Miss
Minturn, Mrs. R. B.
Minturn, Master R. S.

*Norrie, Adam
Norwood, Carlisle Jr.

Otto, Mme. Antoinette
*Osgood, Mrs. S. S.
*Osgood, S. S.
*O'Brien, Wm. & John
*O'Gorman, Richard
*Oothout, William

*Parish, Daniel
*Packer, Daniel
Park, Joseph, Jr.
Perry, Oliver H.
Perry, Mrs. O. H.
Perry, Myrom
Phenix, Phillips
*Pomeroy, Adams & Co.
Purser, George H.
*Pell, Mrs. Mary R.
Parsons, W. H. & Bro.
*Phipps, W. H.
*Phelps, Royal
*Phelps, Dodge & Co.
Partridge, Leroy C.
Palmer, Thomas Jr.

*Roberts, Marshall O.
*Roosevelt, C. V. S.
Roosevelt, J. A.
Rosa, Dr. W. V. V.
Roosevelt, Theodore
*Robbins, George A.
Reed, Isaac H.
*Richardson, Geo. C. & Co.

Robbins, Chandler
Richardson, William
Rivinius, Charles
Reid Walter

Steele, Edward G.
Shaw, Mrs. F. G.
Schenck, Edward
*Stuart, R. L. & A.
*Stewart, A. T.
Spies, Adam ,W.
*Sucley, Rutseen
*Stebbins, Henry G.
*Spotts & Hawk
*Stevens, Paran
Sherman, E. T.
*Stokes, James
*Skinner, F. & Co.
*Stanfield,Wentworth & Co.
*Spaulding, Hunt & Co.
Sands, Samuel S.
*Sweeney, Peter B.
*Sherman, W. Watts
Shook, Sheridan
Singer Manufacturing Co.
Schell, Edward
*Schell, Richard
*Squier, E. George
Sistare, George K., Jr.
*Schemerhorn, W. C.
Schemerhorn, Alfred
Suydam, D. Lydig
Schieferdecker, C. C.
Sullivan, Thomas
Strong, Demas
Solomon, Barnett L.
Solomon, Judah H.
Stacy, George
Solomon, Isaac S.
Strauss, Joseph
Smith, E. L.

Solomons, Moses

Taylor, Moses
Taggart, Robert
*Tiffany, Charles L.
Tilford, John M.
Tousey, Sinclair
Townley, D. O. C.
*Tweed, Wm. M.
*Tilden, S. J.
Thorne, Jonathan
Tompkins, E. H.
Trevend, Mrs.

Van Schaick, Edwin H.
Van Rensselaer, Alex.
Vanderbilt, Jacob H.

*Wolfe, John D.
*Webb, Wm. H.
*Winthrop, B. R.
*Wood, C. B.
Wells, Henry
*Walker, Mrs. John
Williams, John Earle
Wheatley, William
Whetten, Wm.
*Weston, Mrs. R. W.
Wright, Stephen M.
*Wilson, J. F., M. D.
Wallace, Mrs. C. D.
*Ward, Samuel W. H.
*Winslow, Lanier & Co.
*Weston, R. Warren
Wells, Philip
Woodward, G. M.
Westervelt, T.
Welton, Miss C. J.
White, Dr. J. J. P.
Woods, Hon. William
Wagstaff, A.
Young, Miss

Contributions amounting to Five Thousand Dollars, collected from the following, by Horace B. Claflin, Esq.

Claflin, H. B.
Claflin, H. B., Jr.
Chittenden, S. B.
Hoyt, Spragues & Co.
Seligman, J. & W.
Low, Harriman & Co.
Anthony & Hall
Babcock, Bros. & Co.
Little, James L. & Co.
Chase, Stewart & Co.
Howe, J. C. & Co.
Butterfield, Jacobus & Co.
Kutter, Luckemeyer & Co.
Aldrich, Iddings & Clifton.

Paton & Co.
Wright, J. S. & E.
Leland, Allen & Bates
Strong, W. S. & Co.
Demy, Poor & Co.
Slade, John & Co.
Eldridge, Dunbarn & Co.
Stanfield, Wentworth & Co.
Seth B. Hunt & Co
Spaulding, Hunt & Co.
Parker, Wilder & Co.
Harding, Colby & Co.
Langley, W. G. &. Co.
Van Valkenburgh & Haines

Obituary Record.

During the year the Society has to mourn the loss of the following Members:

GEORGE DEXTER,

JOSEPH SAMPSON,

J. A. CLARKE,

THOS. H. FAILE,

RICHARD FRENCH,

HORACE GREELEY,

WILLIAM BLACK,

GEORGE T. TRIMBLE,

JOHN D. WOLFE,

ROBERT J. DILLON,

JAMES GORDON BENNETT.

CONTENTS.

ILLUSTRATIONS.

www.ingramcontent.com/pod-product-compliance
Lightning Source LLC
Chambersburg PA
CBHW031452270326
41930CB00007B/961